Whole-Hearted Work

Nate Holdridge

Published by nateholdridge.com, 2022.

While every precaution has been taken in the preparation of this book, the publisher assumes no responsibility for errors or omissions, or for damages resulting from the use of the information contained herein.

WHOLE-HEARTED WORK

First edition. June 2, 2022.

Copyright © 2022 Nate Holdridge.

ISBN: 979-8201566203

Written by Nate Holdridge.

Table of Contents

To the hard-working people of Calvary Monterey. Thank you for serving our community well.

Chapter 1. Why Work Matters

———

Then God said, "Let us make man in our image, after our likeness. And let them have dominion over the fish of the sea and over the birds of the heavens and over the livestock and over all the earth and over every creeping thing that creeps on the earth." So God created man in his own image, in the image of God he created him; male and female he created them. And God blessed them. And God said to them, "Be fruitful and multiply and fill the earth and subdue it, and have dominion over the fish of the sea and over the birds of the heavens and over every living thing that moves on the earth." (Genesis 1:26–28, ESV).

Why a Series on Work?

Thank you for reading this short book, *Whole-Hearted Work*. In this first chapter, we will consider why work matters. In chapter two, we will consider why work is hard. Then we will think about how to do good work, and conclude with a chapter about work and trust in God.

But why should we take the time to read about work? I hope this first chapter will give you a detailed answer, but my deepest motivation is pastoral. When I consider all the Bible has to say about our professional or personal work, and when I think about the people I am called to serve, I am compelled to talk a bit more about the theology of work.

Even a cursory reading of the letters of the New Testament makes it clear that God is concerned with how we conduct our work. For instance, in multiple letters, Paul instructed both the workers and management represented in the churches he served (Ephesians 6:5-9, Colossians 3:22-4:1). In other letters, he rebuked those who could work but were unwilling to do so, telling them to start working quietly and providing for themselves and their dependents (1 Thessalonians 4:8-12, 2 Thessalonians 3:6-12, 1 Timothy 6:6-10). He even wrote a letter settling a dispute between a servant and his master (Philemon).

Other New Testament authors chimed in as well. James instructed the rich in this present age to conduct and plan their business pursuits while considering God's sovereignty (James 4:13-17). Peter told the church that the way they worked was a witness to Jesus' lordship of their lives and a way to imitate Jesus' example (1 Peter 3:18-25). And John instructed the church to use their paychecks to—in part—support missionaries (3 John).

Scanning these truths of Scripture is enough to stir me up to instruct you about your work life, but the word also directly tells pastors to do so. After teaching about proper Christian workplace dynamics, Paul told Pastor Timothy and all future pastors, *"Teach and urge these things"* (1 Timothy 6:2). God knows that what we do at work occupies so much time, energy, and thought that it benefits us to take some time to consider it all through the lens of Scripture.

The truth is that I probably do not understand your job or career very well, just as you likely do not understand mine. But the word of God applies to all of us regarding the work of our hands, and I hope to draw from biblical texts that will help us grow in our workplace ministry.

WHOLE-HEARTED WORK

Work Defined

At this point, some of you may feel that this book is not for you.

- Perhaps your work is the unpaid kind—caring for a family member, staying at home to parent young children or volunteering—but I assure you that I am thinking of your work also. God was and is a worker, but no one has ever paid him for it.

- Perhaps you no longer work—you have retired, or hardship has forced you to stop working—but you still have work to do in your daily life. Plus, you have others to mentor or encourage, and they will likely work, so it will be helpful for you to think about these concepts.

- Perhaps you are only a student and think a career is something in the future that you do not need to think too seriously about today—but for now, your work is (primarily) the pursuit of your education. And many of you will need to work to support yourself while in school. So this book applies to you today, but also to ready you for tomorrow. It is better to prepare for the future biblically than delay thinking about these concepts until after you are already on your career path.

I realize that for most people throughout history and today, the question of why work matters is a simple one. The answer? Survival. Most of the world's population, even today, just does what there is to be done to eat and drink and be sheltered for another day. It is a relatively privileged position to sit back and ask these larger questions about work and why it matters in God's sight, and it is a privilege that we should determine to use for God's glory and purposes. So let us consider why work matters by drawing on five lessons from Genesis 1:26-28.

Because It Is Godly

God Works

The first reason work matters is because work is godly. The passages surrounding Genesis 1:26-28 bear this out. During the six days of Genesis 1, God worked by creating. He spoke, he named, he thought, and he made distinctions and categories. God worked. He made useful materials for human flourishing, fine-tuning a planet for our enjoyment and cultivation. He made species after species, and then he made us.

And after the six days were over, *"God blessed the seventh day and made it holy, because on it he rested from all his work that he had done in creation"* (Genesis 2:3). Then he put Adam in the garden to work the land (Genesis 2:15). This context shows us God as a worker, and since our passage tells us we are made in his image and are called to imitate him, we should work.

The concept of God as the first worker is crucial because we are prone to make a false distinction between sacred and secular activities. In this view, things like church attendance, prayer, and Bible study are sacred and godly, while things like education, earning wages, or careers are secular and human. But Genesis shows us a God who does work and then invites his people to work as he does.

Jesus

WHOLE-HEARTED WORK

This portrayal of God as a worker is a major difference between Christianity and other world religions that consider working a necessary evil and something to escape in the afterlife. In contrast, the Bible heralds work as good and vital, especially in Christ's incarnation. In John, Jesus said, *"My Father is working until now, and I am working"* (John 5:17).

When God became one of us, what did he look like? A mystic who lived in isolation? A monk who lived in a monastery? An academic who lived in a library? No! When God came as a man, he served a small town in the northern hills of Israel as its carpenter.

Think of it! Jesus came, grew, apprenticed, and learned carpentry from his father. Then he worked that ordinary job for years before his extraordinary public ministry. And in a world dominated by Greek thought and the Roman way of life, Jesus' embrace of hard, manual labor was revolutionary.

As Ben Witherington wrote in his excellent book on the theology of work:

> "The wealthy Roman upper classes in Jesus' day had an aversion to dirty jobs, the kind that get your hands and clothes soiled. Not so ancient Jews like Jesus and Paul, who saw the dignity in manual labor of all sorts. Paul had no problem with being a tentmaker or leatherworker. Jesus had no problem with being a carpenter. Neither should we."—Ben Witherington, Work: A Kingdom Perspective on Labor, pg. 15, loc. 384

We are created in God's image to express what God is like to all of creation, and as Christians, we are called to imitate God, and we work because it is Godlike (Ephesians 5:1).

Because of Christ's Kingdom

The King Must Have a Kingdom

A second reason work matters is because of Christ's kingdom. In Genesis 1:26–28, God said, *"Let us make man in our image,"* and then told us to subdue the earth and have dominion over it. These last exhortations help us make sense of what it means to bear God's image.

In ancient times, when a king conquered a distant land, they would put images of themselves in those lands to remind the populace of their authority. Similarly, God is King overall, including the distant land of planet earth. His people are meant to depict his authority and dominion through the grace-filled way they live their lives. Our self-restraint, kindness, generosity, love, and affinity for the truth are all ways to represent the God who is King.

Unfortunately, God's image in humanity has been marred by sin. Romans say that we have suppressed the truth about God, a truth that echoes in every human heart (Romans 1:16-32). So, in a sense, we are not able to imagine God anymore. Fortunately, Jesus came, and with him, he brought a kingdom. Remember his proclamation early in the gospels? *"The kingdom of God is at hand. Repent and believe in the gospel"* (Mark 1:15). Jesus came for us, suffered and died for us, and rose for us so that if we believe in him, we will come into his kingdom.

WHOLE-HEARTED WORK

Christians consider themselves citizens of Christ's kingdom, right now, today. And what does our King say to us about the way we work? Things like:

> *"Whatever you do, work heartily, as for the Lord and not for men, knowing that from the Lord you will receive the inheritance as your reward. You are serving the Lord Christ."*
> (Colossians 3:23–24)

Because God made us in his image, told us to have dominion to represent his image, and died and rose for us to restore his image in us, our work can be a way to live out his kingdom. We consider the resurrected Jesus to be King over all of life, and this means believers see themselves working and doing all their tasks directly for Jesus. This makes sense because Jesus is the Redeeming God; he can take even the most mundane tasks and redeem them into a chance to express his kingdom here on earth.

This point is important because many have adopted a part-time Christian perspective. When engaged in church activities, when talking to the pastor, or when attending your small group, you adopt certain customs and practices. Then you take those off while you work. But Christ's gospel and leadership are so good they demand our every moment. Let us ditch the part-time Christian perspective and see our work environment as another place his kingdom is expanding.

Work With Christ as King

This point also draws out the concept that some types of work are not compatible with Jesus' kingdom. We might quickly think of some prominent lines of work that are opposite his values. Careers and businesses that entangle people in sexual sin, substance abuse, or financial greed and ruin, for instance, cannot coexist with his kingdom and values. For example, I noticed Netflix is running a documentary about the highly sexualized and racist way a prominent clothing line built its popularity in the early 2000s. A believer in that environment would have to ask hard questions about their involvement or, at the very least, work hard to combat the direction the company was heading.

Let us be people who represent King Jesus in our workplaces. And rather than seeing your work exclusively as a place to get your provision, see it as a place to express your passion. Rather than see it as mundane, see it as a ministry. Rather than impacting no one in your work, see it as a place to impact others for Christ. Rather than choose work that destroys or hurts others, let us choose work that creates and helps others.

Because of Love

The third reason work matters is because of love. Again, God made us to image him throughout the world. The Bible teaches that God is love, so when Christ saves us, the Spirit begins to help us express God's love as a way to image him in our world. Because God is love and we are made in his image, our work should be a vehicle for loving others.

To be loving, of course, is Christ's desire for us. He said the greatest commandment was to love God with all our heart, mind, soul, and strength, but also that we should love our neighbor as we love ourselves (Mark 12:30-31). We have already thought for a bit about how our work can be a way to respect and love God. So how can our work also be a way to love our neighbor?

By Providing for Yourself and Others

When you work well, you provide for yourself and others, which is a way to love others. First, since you have provided for yourself, no one else has to care for you, which makes their burden lighter. Second, when you work to provide for others, you are making the burden of that person and the society around them lighter as well. Jesus told us to feed the hungry, clothe the naked, and serve the sick. Naturally, we think of these as charitable acts, but every new parent has also seen how their love for their child demands that they provide for their food, clothing, and health.

Have you ever thought about how our work provides for others beyond our family or through our generosity? When you work, you are helping provide for your boss and fellow workers. Hopefully, you are producing something of value that helps your fellow man. So your work should be seen as a way to provide not only for yourself but for others as well.

As a pastor, I am often conscious of this in my own work. I depend on my colaborers in many ways, and they depend on me. If I work diligently and wisely on my role in the church, it helps provide for their needs and vice versa. If I were to stop working hard at sermon preparation or leadership, it would harm them, so one way for me to love them is by working hard in my areas of responsibility.

By Building a Society

Another way your work is love for your neighbor is because it builds your society. When the quality of our work improves goods and services, the quality of life increases for everyone else.

Society building is an excellent way for us to, as Paul said, remember the poor (Galatians 2:10). It is undoubtedly good and Christian to pursue the short-term solution of giving food and clothing to those in need. But quality work and enterprise produce goods, jobs, and services over the long term, and this society-building work is a solid way to love others. For instance, when Christian business owners pay their employees a competitive wage or give them good benefits, they express Christ's love to their neighbors.

By Considering the Ramifications of Your Work

Another way your work can be love for your neighbor is when you think of the ramifications of your work. Is your work or career thinking about future generations? What is the impact of your work on the world at large?

Some businesses prey on people's desire for fleeting happiness and encourage them to rack up crippling debt. Some businesses prey on people's insecurities to sell them things they don't even need. Some businesses prey on people's laziness and cause them to waste their lives away. We live in a broken and fallen world, and no business will always represent God's kingdom values, but Christians should consider the ramifications of their role and work.

I have especially appreciated how many social media companies like Facebook, Instagram, YouTube, and others have been called out lately for the tactics they use to foster addiction to their services. In their business model, the product is your attention, and their customers are ad-buyers. And what we are becoming as a result of all our time online is not good. The ramifications of that business model are often harmful. Christians working in companies like these, and in all areas of the workforce, need to think through how their work impacts others.

While considering the ramifications of our work, some of you might be thinking about businesses that harm the environment. While God ordained it that we subdue the earth and form God's raw creation for human flourishing, we should not ruin God's raw creation either. People are sensitive to this today. Many have erred on the side of worshipping the creation. Many others have erred on the side of carelessness. But we are not meant to worship or be at one with creation, nor are we to ruin and destroy it. We should instead cultivate it like managers with a stewardship. This takes wisdom and self-restraint, at times, and sacrifice and responsible development at others.

By Testifying of Christ

Another way to love others with our work is by testifying about Christ in our workplaces. It might be appropriate to hold lunchtime Bible studies or prayer meetings with other Christians in some workplace environments. In others, there might be time to have warm and kind conversations about Christ while working. And in others, it might be only the quality of our work and the character of our person that is allowed to speak of Jesus. Over time, if you do good work, when people discern you are a Christian, they will appreciate what your Christianity has done to you and for your work.

There will always be hostility against Christ in the world. But sometimes, the quality of our work will disarm that hostility. As Peter said, *"This is the will of God, that by doing good you should put to silence the ignorance of foolish people"* (1 Peter 2:15).

Our work is a way to love others when it provides for ourselves and others and helps build society, and when we consider the ramifications of our work, and through our testimony about Christ at our work.

Because It Sanctifies

What Is Sanctification?

Another reason work matters is because it sanctifies. Sanctification is the process Christians enter into after being justified. It begins after we are saved through the gospel of Christ by becoming recipients of the righteousness of Christ. Before God, we have Jesus' standing.

This does not mean we are like Jesus in the way we live. Christlikeness becomes the aim of the Spirit in us, and sanctification is the process he uses to accomplish this goal. Christians are supposed to submit their bodies to this process to experience this change. For instance, Paul said:

> *"I appeal to you therefore, brothers, by the mercies of God, to present your bodies as a living sacrifice, holy and acceptable to God, which is your spiritual worship. Do not be conformed to this world, but be transformed by the renewal of your mind, that by testing you may discern what is the will of God, what is good and acceptable and perfect."* (Romans 12:1–2)

WHOLE-HEARTED WORK

Because we are made in his image, but lost that image through the fall and are regaining that image through Christ's gospel and work, we should expect to be sanctified while we work.

Workplace Sanctification

Think about it—work is where we spend a massive portion of our lives. The way we work, our understanding of our identity as we work, our motivation for our work, and the character we demonstrate at work all contribute to shaping us to be more like Jesus. All-day long, we will be given opportunities to imitate Christ.

Sometimes people say marriage is not meant for happiness but for holiness. It is a little cheeky, but the idea is that entering into marriage is a surefire way to have all of your flaws and sins confronted. And work does this as well. Do you struggle to trust God? At work, you will need to trust God for guidance, to provide, and for results—especially when you refuse to behave in ungodly ways there.

Do you need to grow in patience? At work, you will need the patience to handle the authority above you, coworkers next to you, and employees who follow you. Do you battle greed for more and more? At work, you will be challenged to set boundaries so you don't overwork, find contentment with the wages and earnings due to you, and make decisions that are not unadvisedly aggressive because of the possible payout.

Over and over again, our work will provide character-shaping experiences. Think of a mother doing the hard work of raising young children who likely do not thank her often for her tireless work.

But that stretching experience can deepen her character and Christlikeness.

This sanctification is not automatic. If we do not intentionally commit our days and work to him, we will not be formed into his image. If we do not enter into each meeting, shift, or client meeting with a sense of his presence, Christlikeness will not come. Instead, we will spend every day becoming unlike him because our work has the power to deform us as well. We need the Spirit's power, a daily walk with Christ, and tons of confession and prayer for this sanctification to occur.

It Is Forever

Remembered Forever

One more way our work matters: it is forever. The way we work today matters for tomorrow. Because we are made in God's image, because God expressed dominion over his creation, and because God invited us to have dominion over and subdue the earth, we should expect that even a cup of cold water given in his name will be remembered forever (Matthew 10:42).

> Everyone will be forgotten, nothing we do will make any difference, and all good endeavors, even the best, will come to naught. Unless there is God. If the God of the Bible exists, and there is a True Reality beneath and behind this one, and this life is not the only life, then every good endeavor, even the simplest ones, pursued in response to God's calling, can matter forever.—Timothy Keller, Every Good Endeavor: Connecting Your Work to God's Work

WHOLE-HEARTED WORK

Working Forever

Not only can our work matter forever, but we will also work forever. My reading of the final chapters of Revelation—chapters filled with talk of Christ's reign on earth followed by a new heaven and new earth—is that much work will be done for all of eternity. We are pictured as ruling and building nations and societies there. There is a reason Christ's coming will cause us to beat our swords into plowing instruments (Isaiah 2:4). In heaven, there will be no more war. There will be holy, sweatless, and productive work.

I think this makes perfect sense: because we are made in God's image, because God works, and because God never changes, we should expect to imitate God by working forever. God is love, and he calls us to love. Paul said we should continue in faith, hope, and love while acknowledging love is greater than faith and hope (1 Corinthians 13:13). But why is love the greatest? One reason is that love lasts forever. In eternity God's people will not need faith and hope because we will see God, and in him, our hopes will be fulfilled. But we will love forever. And love requires work, energy, creativity, and focus, so it makes sense that we would have some semblance of work forever with God.

In one way, our work today is designed to create hope in us for that perfect day with perfect work. For all of our best achievements today, the work of our hands is often beset with error, sin, failures, imperfection, and chaos. We have all had days where we wonder if we accomplished anything of value. But those moments should stir in us a hope for the work we will do in glory with him. It will be work that just works!

Chapter 2. Why Work Is Hard

———

And to Adam he said, "Because you have listened to the voice of your wife and have eaten of the tree of which I commanded you, 'You shall not eat of it,' cursed is the ground because of you; in pain you shall eat of it all the days of your life; thorns and thistles it shall bring forth for you; and you shall eat the plants of the field. By the sweat of your face you shall eat bread, till you return to the ground, for out of it you were taken; for you are dust, and to dust you shall return." (Genesis 3:17–19, ESV).

Now that we have considered why work matters, we need to think about the difficulty of work. Why is work hard? Why are even the most fulfilling careers filled with disappointment and brokenness? Why does it feel so hard to provide enough, even in one of the most affluent times and places in history? Why is progress and success at work sometimes hard to come by?

This passage gives us the main answer to these questions. I will try to show you two reasons work is hard in this text, followed by our main solution.

Because of Original Sin

Work Became Painful

The first reason work is hard is because of original sin. Let me explain. Our Bible passage for this chapter (Genesis 3:17-19) could not be more different from the one we studied in the first chapter (Genesis 1:26-28). There, God said he would make humanity in his image to fill the earth, have dominion on the earth, and subdue the earth for their purposes. In this passage, humanity's glory and dominion have clearly been lost. What happened?

Sin happened. After God made the perfect world and after he set his people in the garden to tend and keep it, temptation led our oldest ancestors astray. God had given them unparalleled freedom to enjoy and rule over his creation, but there was one thing they were not to do, one tree they were not to eat from lest death enter the universe. It was a test of their hearts. And it was a test they failed.

The sin Adam committed in the garden is often called original sin, and it has been passed down to all of us. The Bible teaches that because Adam sinned, we all are considered to have sinned with him. So when we were born, we were born in sin. We can argue against that reality, but it is still reality. None of us have proven otherwise, for we all follow up being born in sin by growing up to engage in sin. But the bad news that we are counted with Adam sets up the good news that we can be counted with Jesus. Because Jesus died and rose, we can all be identified with him. Just as we received Adam's unrighteousness, we can receive Jesus' righteousness (see Romans 5:12-21).

But after Adam's sin, God came and told them what the world would be like until Christ renewed it—childbirth became painful, men and women would struggle against each other, and even the ground was cursed. When sin entered the world, everything changed, including our relationship with work.

Because of original sin, work became painful. So when God said, **"Cursed is the ground because of you; in pain you shall eat of it**

all the days of your life," the natural order was overturned (Genesis 3:17). We were meant for dominion, called by God to fill the earth and subdue it. We were going to create societies that glorified God in every way, and the creation was going to cooperate with our godly and good ambitions. But original sin overturned both our ambitions and creation's cooperation. Now work is a war. God said we would eat, but only by the sweat of our brow (Genesis 3:19). We do not have easy dominion over the ground, but now the ground subjects us to a painful struggle to extract food from it. And this pain remains today.

Work Became Frustrating

Because of original sin, work also became frustrating. God said, **"Thorns and thistles it shall bring forth for you"** (Genesis 3:18). These thorns and thistles were something new—they did not exist in the garden of Eden, but with sin came the frustration of thorns and thistles.

And these thorns and thistles are meant to point to a larger reality. Any task we set out to accomplish is beset with some failure. Just as real thorns and thistles are a frustrating experience for the farmer, so proverbial thorns and thistles hinder every work experience. Even when we do everything right, our work is subject to outside, frustrating factors. Even when you are satisfied with the quality of your work, you will not always be satisfied with the results of your work.

Let us imagine a new golf course and country club attached to it. The ownership has a good plan and hires a renowned designer to plot out eighteen holes on the land they have acquired. They design a spectacular facility for potential members. They go through the painstaking process of permitting and building. They hire a great CEO and head golf professional, and together they build an incredible team ready to serve club members. Soon, word gets out, and memberships start rolling in. Everything is looking good, but then some bull-headed and obnoxious members wriggle onto the board and begin challenging the staff. Soon, quality people are driven out of their positions, the atmosphere becomes tense, and the club cannot live up to its potential. Frustrating events like these play out in workplaces all over the world every day, and they can all be traced to the presence of original sin.

I mean, did you hear about CNN+? They spent somewhere around $300M to launch a standalone streaming service but released it right before new owners took over the company. And in less than a month, the entire service was discontinued. All that effort. All that expense for nothing. Work is frustrating.

Remember Nehemiah? He was at the top of his game when he led the people to rebuild the city of Jerusalem, but for all his efforts, the people still struggled to follow him towards godliness. I do not think any of us would blame Nehemiah for that, but if we were in Nehemiah's shoes, we might be tempted to blame ourselves. Sometimes, however, work does not work out because original sin frustrates it.

This truth serves as a helpful alert: just because our work is frustrating does not mean we have chosen the wrong line of work or have the wrong job in that career. It might be a clue, but there is no unicorn career that will be without thorns and thistles. You will never have a job void of some level of frustration. You can be right where God wants you to be, but you will still be frustrated quite often by and in your work. And just because you are not at the very top of your field does not mean you are not right where God has you.

Work Became Futile

And there is more. Because of original sin, work became futile. God said, **"By the sweat of your face you shall eat bread, till you return to the ground, for out of it you were taken; for you are dust, and to dust you shall return"** (Genesis 3:19). So how long would humanity have to toil in the way God described? Until the very ground that rebelled against them consumed them. Until they were buried in and decomposed back into that ground. Until death.

This statement speaks to the perceived futility of life. Day after day and year after year, we work to scratch out a living. And then we die, returning to the dust. King Solomon put on his philosopher hat to write Ecclesiastes. He toiled and worked. His conclusion?

> *"What has a man from all the toil and striving of heart with which he toils beneath the sun? For all his days are full of sorrow, and his work is a vexation. Even in the night his heart does not rest. This also is vanity."* (Ecclesiastes 2:22–23)

Work is not part of the curse - it was part of God's original creation. But work feels the effects of original sin and leads to futile living. Because of the fall, we fight to provide and also to keep the main things main.

This is not hard to illustrate in our current moment. Though we live in a time of massive physical and intellectual advancements and have more health, more knowledge, and more ease than ever before, but we continue suffering in the areas that truly matter. Socially, emotionally, and spiritually, we are hurting. We know that healthy relationships are good for us, but we have a hard time forging them. We know our emotional health is key, but we engage in thought patterns that harm us from within. And we know our spiritual health is important, but we have a hard time connecting with God. So even though we have made massive physical and intellectual strides, we do not seem to be doing much better because the most important things about us are often neglected.

And work's futility often exacerbates these problems. Where is the time, energy, or mental space for relational, emotional, and spiritual health? For many of us, this fallen workplace environment takes so much of it from us.

And work also feels even more futile when we consider the disparity in reward for various forms of work. Surgeons and the U.S. president earn far less than movie stars and athletes. Even if we understand the economic reasons for such disparity, we struggle to think it is right and justified. Futile.

On top of all this is the very real sense that there is no point. Without God, what reason and purpose do we have to work as we do? All this to say, work is hard because of original sin.

Because of Personal Sin

Work is also hard because of personal sin. If original sin altered work's landscape, individual sin populated it. How so?

Sloth: My Work Does Not Matter

WHOLE-HEARTED WORK

One way personal sin makes work hard is through sloth. The slothful person believes their work does not matter. Sometimes their slothful attitude will present itself as physical laziness, but it always treats meaningful and important things as meaningless and unimportant. And work is meaningful and important. But the slothful person does not treat it this way.

The Proverbs have a lot of interesting things to say about someone dominated by sloth. They call this person a "sluggard." Let us consider a few:

> *"Like vinegar to the teeth and smoke to the eyes, so is the sluggard to those who send him."* (Proverbs 10:26)

This first proverb means that the sluggard is annoying to his employers. Working with him is like drinking vinegar or having smoke blown in your eyes. Irritating. As believers, we must recognize we are capable of the sin of sloth. We should want the opposite to result from our lives—for our employers to feel it is a delight to work with us.

> *"The sluggard does not plow in the autumn; he will seek at harvest and have nothing."* (Proverbs 20:4)

At the end of this book is a bonus chapter that fleshes out this second proverb, but for now, we need to know it means the sluggard will not do the preparatory work required to experience a fruitful impact later on. He might have had a vision for the good life and he may have wanted a harvest, but he got none because he did not plow in the autumn. As believers, we should become willing to work hard in advance so that long-term fruit can come. We get our education. We plan. We prepare. We put in the work just like Jesus did. And like Jesus, we enjoy the harvest when it is time.

> *"The sluggard says, 'There is a lion in the road! There is a lion in the streets!' As a door turns on its hinges, so does a sluggard on his bed. The sluggard buries his hand in the dish; it wears him out to bring it back to his mouth. The sluggard is wiser in his own eyes than seven men who can answer sensibly."* (Proverbs 26:13–16)

This third cluster of proverbs means that the sluggard is full of wild excuses to keep from working—*"there's a lion out there somewhere!"* It also means that he loves sleep way too much—*"as a door turns on its hinges, so does a sluggard on his bed."* It also means that even the most menial tasks knock him off course—he cannot even deal with feeding himself! And it also means that he has an exalted view of his opinion on things, thinking himself wiser than plenty of others who have answered sensibly.

In some ways, in our modern and western world, people can be lazier than they have ever been. As believers, we do not make excuses for ourselves but recognize that, like Jesus, we must do hard things. As believers, we do not lounge around and let life pass us by, but we get up and engage in Jesus' plans for us. As believers, we do not despise the small and menial tasks because we follow a Savior who came and served people no one else wanted to serve. And as believers, we do not think we have all the answers but that they are found in God, so we humbly learn and listen.

Pride: My Work Really Matters

Another way personal sin makes work hard is through pride. If the slothful man says his work does not matter, the prideful man says his work really matters. This pride can show up in a number of ways.

Our work can foster pride in us when we use it as a way to feel secure. It is tempting to trust our work to care for us in a way that only God can. As James said, *"Come now, you who say, 'Today or tomorrow we will go into such and such a town and spend a year there and trade and make a profit'— yet you do not know what tomorrow will bring. What is your life? For you are a mist that appears for a little time and then vanishes. Instead you ought to say, 'If the Lord wills, we will live and do this or that'"* (James 4:13–15). James' idea is that since only God knows what tomorrow holds, only God can be trusted with tomorrow.

Our work can also foster pride in us when we use it as a way to enjoy power and status of some kind. You do not have to be a CEO of a large company to feel this temptation, either. Even an anonymous administrative worker can become a gatekeeper exerting authority over others.

Our work can also foster pride in us when we use it as a form of identity. God said we should have no other gods before him, but work and career can become a god we use to tell us who we are. But this makes work an idol of the heart.

> *"Idolatry means imagining and trusting anything to deliver the control, security, significance, satisfaction, and beauty that only the real God can give. It means turning a good thing into an ultimate thing."* — Andrew Peterson, Adorning The Darkness

As believers, we must know that our work cannot justify us. Jesus justifies us by his blood. We cannot work for salvation. Instead, work is meant to be a tool we use to worship God and represent him well here on earth.

Jesus Can Help Us

All this despair could crush us. But instead, we should allow it to drive us to Christ and his gospel. Work is hard because of original sin and personal sin, but Jesus can help us. Because Jesus died on the cross to deliver us from sin, we are not doomed to a deadly spiral in our work. In Christ, the effects of the fall are diminished and will ultimately be destroyed. Right now, the gospel of Jesus Christ can transform our work out of the effect sin has on it. Let me point out two ways.

Purpose

First, Jesus can give your work purpose. Work was supposed to be a love response to God's love. In the garden, that is what it was. The fall removed us from God's presence and the experience of God's love, but the cross releases God's love on us once again. So now we can get back on track to love God through our work. Jesus redeemed us, bought us out of sin's slavery, and his redemptive ministry affects our work as well.

> *"Whatever you do, work heartily, as for the Lord and not for men."* (Colossians 3:23)

To work with the aim of pleasing Christ should help us do better at choosing satisfying work. We have more power to choose our work today than ever before. Hardly anyone picks up the trade their father did anymore. We have many choices when it comes to work. And if it does not work out, there is always another option right around the corner! Despite this, many people are dissatisfied with the work they have chosen.

Jesus can help us with this because he redeems work. In Christ, we are free to please him with any work he has gifted us to do. In Christ, we are free of the pressure to attain status or identity through our work, so we can choose work he would be pleased with. In Christ, we become servants of humanity, which helps us embrace work that benefits others. In Christ, our true satisfaction comes from our relationship with God. And because we do not expect work to complete us, our options can expand. In Christ, we know he is coming to renew all things, so we are released from the pressure to create a perfect society with our work. In Christ, we learn we are one member among billions of his people, and we are set free from the pressure to significantly "change the world" through our work.

Perseverance

Second, Jesus can give you perseverance in your work. Everything we have learned in this chapter helps with this perseverance. We know work will never be perfect because we live in a broken and fallen world. We expect pain and suffering. We are not blind; we know the truth—our work will not always work.

And Jesus' Spirit helps us persevere by strengthening us from within to deal with the multitude of challenging situations and people work throws at us. When we are walking in the Spirit—when we are enjoying God relationally—we will demonstrate love, joy, peace, patience, kindness, goodness, faithfulness, gentleness, and self-control in the workplace (Galatians 5:22-23)

And this perseverance to endure work today is helped by the hope Christians have for tomorrow. We believe a day is coming when we and all of creation will be set free from the effects of the Genesis 3 curse. Listen to Paul:

> *"...the creation was subjected to futility, not willingly, but because of him who subjected it, in hope that the creation itself will be set free from its bondage to corruption and obtain the freedom of the glory of the children of God. For we know that the whole creation has been groaning together in the pains of childbirth until now. And not only the creation, but we ourselves, who have the firstfruits of the Spirit, groan inwardly as we wait eagerly for adoption as sons, the redemption of our bodies."* (Romans 8:20–23)

And it is Jesus who came to make this future hope possible. Everything in our passage today points to him. The death, the toil, the sweat, the thorns, the tree, the temptation... all of it can be traced to Christ. He is the better Adam. He died so we could live. He toiled on our behalf. He sweat great drops of blood in the garden. He wore a crown of thorns. He endured temptation in the wilderness. And he died on a tree.

But Jesus rose, making the way for us to escape all this brokenness and decay forever. The offspring of Eve has arrived to crush Satan under his feet. And one day, work will no longer be hard because Christ will have completely reversed the curse. Let us persevere until that glorious day.

Chapter 3. How To Do Good Work

———

Bondservants, obey in everything those who are your earthly masters, not by way of eye-service, as people-pleasers, but with sincerity of heart, fearing the Lord. Whatever you do, work heartily, as for the Lord and not for men, knowing that from the Lord you will receive the inheritance as your reward. You are serving the Lord Christ. For the wrongdoer will be paid back for the wrong he has done, and there is no partiality. Masters, treat your bondservants justly and fairly, knowing that you also have a Master in heaven. (Colossians 3:22–4:1, ESV).

In 1 Kings 19, one of the great prophets of Israel was looking for his replacement. Elijah was worn out from years of feeling like a lone voice against the sins of Israel's monarchy and people, so God raised up a man named Elisha to take his place. When Elijah recruited to Elisha for the work, Elisha was busy plowing a field with a yoke of oxen. When Elijah offered the job to him, Elisha quickly said goodbye to his parents, sacrificed the oxen, cooked the meat with a fire he made out of their wooden yokes, gave the meat to the townspeople, and arose to leave town with Elijah.

In our last chapter on why work is hard, you might have daydreamed about a similar end to your job. An abrupt end. Burning it all down. Peace out.

I jest, of course, but this is precisely the attitude many Christians have about work and the world as we know it. In a weary world, it is tempting to only look forward to departure, fire, and the end. But can Christ redeem our lives today? Can he infuse our work with meaning and purpose? I think so, and this text points us in this important direction.

Bondservants

The passage is primarily addressed to a group of **bondservants** in the Colossian church (22). These were slaves. And while it is true that their Roman form of slavery was closer to indentured servitude than the horrors of the African slave trade, do not let anyone tell you it was easy. The ideas and implications of the gospel eventually saturated the empire enough to abolish slavery. But in Paul's day, it was still an institution, and Christians needed guidance on how to work in these terrible conditions. And, because their situation was difficult, Paul's guidance to them on how to do good work will also ring true for us. If his exhortations could help navigate slavery, they can certainly help us in our free economy. So what does the passage show us about how to do good work?

Work For Your Master in Heaven

Fearing the Lord

The first way this passage tells us how to do good work is by working for your Master in heaven. This concept is scattered throughout the entire paragraph, as Paul starts by telling the bondservants to **fear the Lord** instead of their **earthly masters** (22). The fear of God is a concept that means to revere God, stand in awe of God, respect God, and ultimately fear a life contrary to or without God. Then Paul doubles down on this concept by telling us to **work for the Lord and not for men** (23). He went on to say that we should see our work as a way we are **serving the Lord Christ** (24). And he even reminded the authority figures in the congregation that they had **a Master in heaven** to whom they must report (1).

In the opening chapter of this book, we thought about how Jesus came with a kingdom and how we are representatives of his reign here on earth. Our work should be done as if King Jesus commissioned us to do it. Here, in this passage, Paul codifies that message. Rather than see ourselves doing our work for earthly employers or authorities, we must believe we are doing our work for King Jesus.

None of this meant that the ancient slaves Paul wrote to were to stop working for their earthly masters, just as none of this means we are to stop working for our employers today. What it means is that the visible authorities in our lives—bosses, employers, leadership—have another authority behind them. We are to see through them and their imperfections to Christ and his perfection. We are to see our work as being done for our Master in heaven.

Do you see what's happening here? Christ is being presented as the redeemer—not only of our spiritual lives, not only of our future with him— but our actual, tangible, physical lives today.

When God created the first man, he put him in the garden to tend and cultivate it. That first instance of work was meant as a way for man to enjoy God. But sin marred the beauty of work. We became separated from God, and work lost its divine touch. Man no longer worked as a form of worship but for survival.

But when Jesus comes into your life, he redeems everything, including work. Now our work can return to a semblance of the worshipful atmosphere originally intended. Will it be perfect? Not yet. But can it be done for and in his name? Yes. And this brings a bit of life back to even the most mundane or frustrating work environments.

Identity

There are two healthy byproducts of the mentality that your work is ultimately for your Master in heaven. The first is that it protects you from getting your identity from your work. It is an inevitable temptation for many of us. Some of us spend so much time preparing for and carrying out our careers that it becomes easy to make our work our identity.

I do not know if you have seen the truck commercial about identity. The truck owner is at a backyard barbeque, and someone asks him, "What do you do?" And his mind flashes, not to his work but to dozens of adventures he has gone on with his truck, camping, rock climbing, off-roading. The implication is that his identity was not in his job but in his lifestyle. Conveniently, his truck brand is willing to sell you a bit of that same lifestyle.

Some of us might think that message is good—*I'm not what I do for work! I am so much more!* It is true. You are. But your work is an important part of you, a gift you give to the world, and a mark you make on society. And the man in the commercial simply found his identity wrapped up in his hobbies and personal interests—good things that cannot ever be God-things. So instead of trying to find your identity in something other than work—adventure guy, workout guy, creative guy, family guy—find your identity in Christ. And because you are working for Christ as your Master in heaven, know your deepest identity is in him, and he asks you to work in his name.

This Destroys Eye-Service and People-Pleasing

The second healthy byproduct of seeing your work as done for King Jesus is the destruction of **eye-service** and **people-pleasing** (22). We know what Paul is alluding to. It is working in a way that calls attention to yourself. It is work that is done only to catch the eye of the boss. It gives effort only when they are watching. And this people-pleasing mentality is a cancer to any workplace.

But seeing Christ as our true Master in heaven, the one we respect and worship, eradicates us of the sin of eye service and men-pleasing. Why? Because Jesus sees us at all times. He is always with us, and he can always weigh the quality of our work.

Allow me to give a brief pep talk on this point. Our Lord and King has commissioned us to work well. He wants students to study hard, be honest, and give their best. He wants employees to work hard, be diligent at all times, and add value to their organization. He wants employers to be just and fair with those they lead. And he is watching our lives, evaluating our work.

Do not let your life pass by while doing subpar work. Do not be a people-pleaser who only does what they can to give the impression they are a good employee. Do not cheat your work by spending time on your phone, wasting time online, or kicking back while on the job. Do not come in to work underslept and unmotivated. Do not bring a bad attitude into the workplace. Christ is on the throne. He is your King. And he demands more from us.

Work With the Right Heart

Genuine and Enthusiastic

The second way this passage shows us how to do good work is by telling us to work with the right heart. When God selected David to be the next king in Israel, he sent Samuel the prophet to the house of Jesse. When Samuel saw David's oldest brother, he was impressed. He thought, *"Surely, the LORD's anointed is before him"* (1 Samuel 16:6). But God had other plans—and he rejected all seven of David's older brothers. God said, *"The LORD sees not as a man sees; man looks on the outward appearance, but the LORD looks on the heart"* (1 Samuel 16:7).

This inward look is God's way. God is always concerned with our heart's motivations. And in this passage, he tells us we should **work heartily** with complete **sincerity of heart** (22-23). What does this mean?

To work with **sincerity of heart** means that we are to work with pure and undivided motives. Our mindset—our inner motivations—should be for the good of our workplaces.

And to **work heartily** in **whatever we do** means that we put our whole heart into our endeavors. Whatever we do—work, school, volunteer—we give our best effort. To work heartily is to approach all forms of your work with enthusiasm.

The genuine and enthusiastic worker will not merely punch the clock or do the minimum. They believe they are created in Christ Jesus for good works, so they work as if their job was one of the good works Jesus had in mind (Ephesians 2:10).

WHOLE-HEARTED WORK

Some of you might feel overwhelmed at this point. Your work is not easy to be enthusiastic about, and your heart is not genuinely interested in what you are being paid to do. We already considered how believing our work is for our Master in heaven can revitalize our motivations, but for you, I would also recommend the words of Jesus in the sermon on the Mount. He said:

> *"Where your treasure is, there your heart will be also."* (Matthew 6:21)

My encouragement—based on this verse—is to begin going through the motions of showing genuine interest and enthusiasm for all your work and watch what happens. Jesus said wherever you put your treasure, your heart follows. My prayer for you is that the motions will turn into emotions and that soon you will find yourself with sincere joy and a real passion for your work.

This biblical attitude is also helpful because it is a key to advancement. Someone disinterested or disengaged from their work is not the first choice for promotion and fresh opportunities. They are not attractive to other prospective employers either. Many employers and leaders are looking less for aptitude and more for attitude. We can learn most of the skills required to do good work, but a good attitude is hard to find. Without a sincere heart and genuine enthusiasm, we will often find ourselves stuck and without opportunities to advance. But with them, doors open.

How Spiritual Disciplines Can Impact Your Heart and (Therefore) Your Work

How do we acquire this sincere and enthusiastic heart? Is there hope for our inner person? Is transformation possible? In Christ, yes.

Through interaction with him, our hearts can be renewed and transformed to be like him. By engaging with him in the ways he has prescribed, we can gain a sincere and enthusiastic heart for our work. What do I mean? Let us consider a handful of biblical spiritual disciplines and how they could impact our hearts for our work.

Your heart would benefit from the spiritual discipline of solitude. While alone with God, he will recharge you for the work you do with others. He will give you clarity on projects and initiatives as you separate yourself and get alone with him. And he will quietly prepare you to have faith and trust in him with your work and in the workplace. Solitude will make you a better worker than those who never take time to slow down, think problems through, and become calmed by the Spirit.

Your heart would also benefit from the spiritual discipline of Bible study. When you meditate upon Scripture, your mentality and character are shaped by its truths. Each day, you will be repointed to larger truths about your coworkers, your mission, and the authority figures in your life. Scripture will make you a better worker than those who listen to fad voices, pseudo-Christian pontificators, or divisive commentators.

Your heart would also benefit from the spiritual discipline of fasting or generosity. I couple these together because they both involve personal sacrifice—doing something that hurts a bit. People who practice self-denial become good at doing hard things. This will make you a better worker than those who regularly avoid pain at all costs.

Your heart would also benefit from the spiritual discipline of Christian fellowship. Christian friends will point you to Christlikeness when all you want to do is complain about, sabotage, or underperform in your workplace. Christian fellowship will make you a better worker than those who are constantly listening to immature or ungodly advice on how to navigate the workplace.

Your heart would also benefit from the spiritual discipline of regular church engagement. When you habitually gather with your church, you are refocused on God. God is constant, reliable, and eternal, and connecting with him helps us with the frenetic, unpredictable, and temporary nature of our work. Regular church engagement will make you a better worker than those whose entire well-being rises and falls with their work successes.

Your heart would also benefit from the spiritual discipline of Sabbath rest. When you take a day each week to enjoy God, his creation, and key relationships, you will be energized for the week to come. Sabbath rest will make you a better worker than those who go hard all weekend and use the workweek for recovery.

So the spiritual disciplines—and all of the Christian life and truth—are beneficial to our work. When we neglect our walk with God, we dry up. Going to work without abiding in Christ means we are giving our workplaces the worst version of ourselves. Instead, we should press into Christ and watch how he transforms us to bless our workplaces.

Believers should go to work with pure motivations. Jesus can shape those motivations, and this shaping often happens as we spend time with him in the ways he has prescribed. All of this will help us work with the right heart.

Work for the Ultimate Reward

The Inheritance

The final way this passage tells us how to do good work is by working for the ultimate reward. To make this point, I need to impress upon you just how shocking the truth Paul proclaimed would have been to his original audience. As slaves, the workers that Paul wrote to did not expect to receive the reward of an inheritance from their masters. Because they were only servants to the household and not members of it, they did not qualify for the inheritance.

But here, the Bible says these slaves needed to **know that from the Lord they would receive the inheritance as their reward** (24). How could this be!? Through the gospel of Jesus Christ, we who were far off are brought near by the blood of Christ (Ephesians 2:13). We are now adopted sons and daughters of God (Romans 8:15-17). We will receive the inheritance of Christ because his blood has brought us into the family of God.

Simultaneous to the joyous truth is a sobering one. Paul said **the wrongdoer will be paid back for the wrong he has done** (25). And, since **there is no partiality with God**, even **masters** should **treat their servants justly and fairly** (25, 1). The idea is that God will both reward his people and judge sinners. All Christians—both those in authority and those who are not—should work as if they will give an account of their lives to God. They should work as if there is a paycheck behind the paycheck, the one coming with Christ at his return.

This word from Paul served as a word of comfort—especially to beleaguered slaves who had little hope for earthly success. One day, Christ would come, and *then* they would get their reward.

A Stewardship Mindset

Perhaps this ultimate and future inheritance reward will motivate us to reverse engineer our lives. What I mean is that we should think more deeply about the brevity of life and how to design our lives in the light of eternity.

And one way to reverse engineer our lives is to work with a stewardship mindset. If Christ has entrusted a level of opportunity, resources, and abilities to us, we must steward them well. If you are a leader, work hard to become a better leader. If you are a parent, work hard to become a better parent. If you are a student, work hard to become a better student. Whatever opportunity we have, we should be faithful to it until the day Christ comes.

In the book of Genesis, Joseph can inspire us to live this way. He was the youngest of all of the sons of Israel, but God gave him dreams that he would one day rule over his brothers and even his parents (Genesis 37:5-11). But when his brothers heard of these dreams and saw the favoritism their father showed Joseph, jealousy drove them to fake his death and sell him into slavery (Genesis 37:12-36). Suddenly, the dreamer was in Egypt, far from home, enslaved.

What did Joseph do? He trusted God and worked as hard as he could for his new master, Potiphar. It came to the point that Potiphar did not even know what was in his bank account—he had grown to trust Joseph that much (Genesis 39:6). And Joseph's presence did nothing but bring blessing upon the entire household (Genesis 39:3, 5).

After a false accusation unfairly landed Joseph in prison, he responded as he did when sold into slavery. He served. He worked. And God blessed everything he did. Soon, the prisoner was running the prison (Genesis 40).

Finally, Pharaoh invited Joseph into his courts because he heard Joseph could interpret dreams. And Pharaoh needed an interpretation of two vivid dreams. Joseph—who had had two vivid dreams of his own many years earlier—gave the interpretation with God's help and ended up serving Pharaoh for many years. The son who became a slave who became a prisoner became the second most powerful man in the world.

But Joseph did this by being a faithful steward of whatever opportunity God put in front of him. I do not think he was happy about each situation he was put in, but he did not grumble either. Instead, he prayed and went to work, asking and expecting God to use him despite his circumstances.

And as he stewarded his opportunities, Joseph kept his mind on the future reward God promised. He never forgot the original dreams God gave him. How do I know? When Pharaoh asked Joseph to interpret his two dreams, Joseph said, *The doubling of Pharaoh's dreams means that the thing is fixed by God, and God will shortly bring it about*" (Genesis 41:32). What faith! We might have expected him to say, *"The doubling of Pharaoh's dreams means God is going to take his sweet time—if he ever moves at all!"* But Joseph did not think that way. He was clinging to the future inheritance God said he would receive. We must have a similar faith while we work, trusting our true reward-inheritance is coming with Christ.

Breathing Life Into Work

One of my favorite stories from the life of Christ is when he raised Lazarus back to life. He was very dead—his death, funeral, and burial had all already occurred. When Jesus commanded them to remove the stone from his tomb, Lazarus' sister objected, *"Lord, by this time there will be an odor, for he has been dead for four days"* (John 11:40). But Jesus is the resurrection and the life, so he insisted. And out came a Lazarus with linen burial strips unraveling from his body. What was dead is now alive!

Perhaps this passage can have a similar effect on your work. You might think it is sucking the life out of you. You might think there is no life in it. You might even think it stinks. But Jesus is the resurrection and the life. He is the great redeemer, and his life can infuse life into your work.

Instead of working for human authorities who will inevitably discourage and disappoint us, Christians work for Christ. Disappointing employees or discouraging employers cannot totally bring us down because we know we are serving Jesus.

Instead of working with disingenuous motives and apathy, Christians work with genuine zeal and enthusiasm. The most mundane tasks become fresh and exciting because we see them as acts of worship to our good Lord.

And instead of working only for material reward today, Christians work for the eternal inheritance that will come with Christ's return.

Even meager rewards and pay push us to look beyond and to the better payment coming with Christ.

But what do we do with ourselves when we fail to live up to the exhortations found in this section of Scripture? We must look past ourselves to the bondservant who did all his Master required. He obeyed all the way to the point of death on a cross (Philippians 2:8), and he did this to intervene for us, a people who were in rebellion against God. He died, and now he lives so that we can be forgiven of any and all violations against the God who made us. We must trust him, receive his forgiveness, and accept his grace to begin again, allowing him to make our workplace a worship space where we follow him.

Chapter 4. Trust God While You Work

My son, do not forget my teaching, but let your heart keep my commandments, for length of days and years of life and peace they will add to you. Let not steadfast love and faithfulness forsake you; bind them around your neck; write them on the tablet of your heart. So you will find favor and good success in the sight of God and man. Trust in the Lord with all your heart, and do not lean on your own understanding. In all your ways acknowledge him, and he will make straight your paths. Be not wise in your own eyes; fear the Lord, and turn away from evil. It will be healing to your flesh and refreshment to your bones. Honor the Lord with your wealth and with the firstfruits of all your produce; then your barns will be filled with plenty, and your vats will be bursting with wine. My son, do not despise the Lord's discipline or be weary of his reproof, for the Lord reproves him whom he loves, as a father the son in whom he delights. (Proverbs 3:1–12, ESV).

The Blessings Mentioned

The promises this passage make sound too good to be true. The author, King Solomon, tells his son about a life that leads to many overlapping blessings. The first blessing is that of **length of days and years of life and peace** (2). The second blessing is that of **favor and good success in the sight of God and man** (4). The third blessing is that of **straightened paths** (6)—obstacles are removed! The fourth blessing is physical and therapeutic well-being—**healing in his flesh and refreshment to his bones** (8). And the fifth and final blessing is prosperity—**barns filled with plenty and vats bursting with wine** (10).

It All Centers on Trusting God

I doubt any of us would deny the appeal of such a life. And would it not be an incredible joy to see the results fleshed out in our work and workplaces? Would it not be beautiful to experience an underlying peace, the removal of obstacles, the enjoyment of spiritual and emotional health, and tangible successes in our work? I think so. But how does Solomon say this brand of life is unlocked? By trusting God. In the middle of this teaching to his son, he said:

> *"Trust in the LORD with all your heart, and do not lean on your own understanding. In all your ways acknowledge him, and he will make straight your paths."* (Proverbs 3:5–6)

This concept is at the center of all these appeals because trust is the heartbeat that steadily pumps these blessings throughout our lives. Without a strong **heart** of trust for God—with a weak trust heartbeat, if you will—the passage's blessings will not be pushed out to the extremities of our lives. But with a heart of trust, a life leaning on God's wisdom rather than our own, great blessings will flow.

In this passage, the word for **"trust"** means "to lie helpless, facedown." It pictures a servant waiting for their master's command or a defeated soldier yielding to a conquering general. We are in a season today when believers need to trust God when it comes to work. Many of us feel like Encyclopedia Britannica door-to-door salesmen in the 90s—the world is changing, and our jobs are changing right along with it! For this, we must trust God.

And this trust for God acknowledges God at all times in **all** our **ways**—including in our work (6). It understands that there are limits to our understanding. It comprehends that God's wisdom is incomprehensible. It agrees with God when he says, *"My thoughts are not your thoughts, neither are your ways my ways. For as the heavens are higher than the earth, so are my ways higher than your ways and my thoughts than your thoughts"* (Isaiah 55:8-9). This brand of trust declares with Paul, *"Oh, the depth of the riches and wisdom and knowledge of God! How unsearchable are his judgments and how inscrutable his ways! For who has known the mind of the Lord, or who has been his counselor?"* (Romans 11:33-34).

As one mature believer told me recently about responsibilities and decisions that were piling up on him: *"Every day, on my calendar, I write the sentence, 'I don't know how.'"* The attitude of faith says, *I do not know how, but I know God, and I trust him.*

If this trust is the center of this passage, we should expect that the truths surrounding it would explain trust. So what does it look like? The truths in this passage provide the color. It is as if trust is the general appeal, but the phrases right before and after it in Solomon's teaching help us understand specific ways to trust God. For our purposes, we will apply these specific ways to trust God in our workplaces.

With Your Character

Steadfast Love and Faithfulness

The first way the text tells us to trust God is with our character. Solomon wanted his son to be shaped by his words. In the opening sentence, he tells his son not to **forget his teaching**, but instead **keep**

his commandments from his **heart** (1). This is at the heart of the Proverbs—this book teaches us how to live a life of skill. Have you heard the saying that it would be better to take time to sharpen your ax than spend all your energy trying to cut down a tree with a dull ax? Proverbs is about sharpening your ax, making life easier because it is now governed by wisdom.

And one of the first things the father tells his son in this passage is to take care of his character. He should **not let steadfast love and faithfulness forsake him, binding them around his neck and writing them on the tablet of his heart** (3). What does this exhortation mean? The young man should always let kindness and truth guide him. He should always be loving and faithful in his life (and work). He should get those attributes deep down into his inner man. He should let them guide his life.

At Work

Trusting God with our character is challenging while we work. It is tempting to think the character God wants us to live with will hurt our work. We might even go so far as to imagine Jesus trying to do our job, believing he would be an utter failure. We envision him getting taken advantage of because he is such a nice and kind servant, getting in trouble for taking long breaks to talk with a hurting coworker, or giving away all the profits. We cannot imagine him being strong enough to handle the rigors our work would throw at him.

But we forget that the job of the Messiah was filled with thousands of pressures, and Jesus managed them all. And before his public ministry, he was the carpenter in Nazareth. Jesus was well acquainted with hard work.

On top of this, the character of Christ is found in many of the heroic workers of Scripture. For instance, in our last chapter, we thought about Joseph from Genesis. Unfairly imprisoned, he worked well and faithfully for his captors and was eventually charged with running the prison. One day, two of Pharaoh's servants were charged with conspiracy and thrown into prison. Each received a vivid dream that meant something, but they did not know what. When Joseph visited them, he saw the sadness on their faces, so he asked them what was wrong (Genesis 40:6-7). That simple question unlocked massive opportunities for Joseph—it was a great career move—but that is not why he asked it. He asked because he was displaying the spirit of Christ. As a God-fearing man, he knew he was called to care for others. It just happened to be a significant aid to his career.

And the Bible is filled with many strong believers who display Christlike character in their workplaces. Daniel held fast to his integrity—he would not compromise his convictions for his boss—and God so blessed him for it that he obtained promotion after promotion. Esther stood up for God and his people, risking her own safety in the process, and God rewarded her with increased influence and security. Nehemiah governed according to biblical principles. Paul worked in anonymity to provide for his needs. Roman military officers led with Christlike sacrifice and cared for others.

But it is all too easy to think that the character God asks of us will not work in our workplaces. Do not give in to that temptation. Instead, trust him with your character.

With Your Abilities

The Growth of Wisdom

We must also trust God with our abilities. Solomon told his son not to be **wise in his own eyes**, but to instead **fear the Lord and turn away from evil** (7). This is an interesting exhortation because of the nature of Proverbs as a book teaching us about the life of skill. When we heed it, our life will inevitably improve. We might even begin to look like we know what we are doing!

So the son was in danger. As he trusted God and received God's wisdom, he might begin thinking the wisdom originated with him. He might become **wise in his own eyes** (7). When he did, he would start committing the sin of Adam and Eve when they stopped thinking about what God said was good and evil but began defining it for themselves.

At Work

As you trust God while you work, make sure you trust him with your abilities. Stay humble and recognize they all come from him. If he gives you a skill, remember it came from him. If he gives you a wise decision, remember it came from him. If he gives you a promotion, remember it came from him.

Do you remember the cautionary story of Samson? God gave him massive and supernatural physical strength so he could be a deliverer of God's people. When they prayed to God for help against their enemies, Samson was designed as a special weapon for God's use. But as Samson's life progressed, he began to forget it all came from God. He became self-assured and strong in his own eyes. One day, when the Philistines attacked, Samson arose to defend himself *"but did not know that the Lord had left him"* (Judges 16:20). His self-assurance ended up being his downfall.

Let us be a people who credit God for our talents, our positions, and our opportunities. We truly could not do what we do without God—he even supplies the air we breathe! So we must trust God with our abilities. Jesus often gave the analogy of a master who went on a long journey. Before he left, he entrusted his staff with various amounts of responsibility and money. When he returned, he was most pleased with the servants who faithfully multiplied his investment. One lesson we should take from these stories is that our Master has given us gifts, talents, and abilities he wants us to use faithfully. But we must never forget that they came from him.

With Your Finances

Shame and Honor

The passage also shows us we must trust God with our finances. Solomon told his son to **honor the Lord with his wealth and with the firstfruits of his produce** (9). In their Old Testament setting, honoring God with their wealth would have included:

- Tithing (giving a tenth to God)

- Sporadic free-will offerings also to God

- Various forms of charitable giving

One specific example is mentioned in the text: giving God the **firstfruits of all their produce**, which was a way for them to recognize all provisions and crops came from God (9).

A major reason we work is to earn money. And money—especially in our work—is another significant area we need to trust God. For many of you, the financial realm is a source of continual stress. You are feeling the pressure—perhaps stronger than ever before—in this modern time. You do not know what you will do for work. Or your job is changing. Or inflation is killing you. Or you are not making enough. Or you are not being compensated fairly. Many factors combine to make money a source of discouragement and frustration for many of us.

All this discouragement and frustration can also lead to a general feeling of guilt or shame regarding money. Many of us are carrying around an internal embarrassment about how we have handled our finances. Perhaps we have heard, thought, or taught things in church settings that make us unsure if money is good or something that God even cares about. Many have misquoted Paul to say money is the root of all evil (rather than "the love of money is a root of all kinds of evils," 1 Timothy 6:10), so many of us are under the impression that money is a sinful or ungodly thing. And many of us have mismanaged our money in some way, and our regret beats us up and makes us feel that when things are financially hard, we are only getting what we deserve.

Perhaps, to remedy our shame, we should know the Bible does not present money as evil. In one sense, money is as good or evil as the person who possesses it. It is what we do with money that is good or evil. In another sense, money is always good in that a monetary system allows us to build societies and improve life together. Without one, we would all still be bartering for goods and services.

But for the shame we might feel, Jesus is inviting us into a fresh supply of his grace and a new start. The passage before us today invites us into such a beginning. Starting today, we can honor God with our wealth. But how?

The Wise Use of Money

First, we can begin using our money well. I encourage every one of you to make a plan or budget for how you will spend, save, and give. John Wesley, the famous eighteenth-century preacher, once said Christians should earn all they can, save all they can, and give all they can. This requires some planning, telling your money where to go.

Second, we can begin working for God first. What I mean is that the theology of work we are developing in this book should help us see money as important, but also secondary to first honoring God with our work and the way we work.

Third, we can practice generosity. Christians are called to use their money to support gospel work—from their local church all the way to foreign soil. We are also called to help with the needs we are exposed to throughout life. When we honor God with our wealth in this way, we gain power over money and the false sense of security it gives us. And since our treasure is with the kingdom, our heart becomes more passionate for the kingdom.

And fourth, we can practice the secret of contentment. Paul said, *"I have learned in whatever situation I am to be content. I know how to be brought low, and I know how to abound. In any and every circumstance, I have learned the secret of facing plenty and hunger, abundance, and need. I can do all things through him who strengthens me"* (Philippians 4:11–13). Perhaps the Spirit of Christ, the one who came from the highest of heights and voluntarily took on the lowest of lows, can help us be content in whatever situation life throws our way.

But, whatever you do, please do not think of earning money in your work as a necessary evil. It is part of God's design for us to live from our work. And the value you produce for yourself is helpful to everyone around you, including your family, your coworkers, and your society. Instead of seeing money as a necessary evil, see it as a good way for humanity to subdue and have dominion on earth as God intended. But be careful not to allow it to become a god that dominates you. Instead, trust God with your finances.

When You Are Disciplined

Sanctification Process

Solomon concludes this mini-teaching with one last area to trust God: trust him when he disciplines you. He told his son not to **despise the Lord's discipline or be weary of his corrective voice, for the Lord reproves those whom he loves, like a father the son in whom he delights** (11-12).

Earlier in this book, we thought about our work as a significant source of personal growth, what the Bible calls sanctification. God often uses workplace challenges to shape us to become more like Jesus. The New Testament book of Hebrews comments on this proverb by saying, *"God disciplines us for our good, that we may share his holiness"* (Hebrews 12:10). This often comes in the form of his discipline or correction for an action or attitude we have displayed in our work.

But we should not despise this corrective work of God. We know we will make mistakes in our work. We will bring our sins and faults and imperfections into the workplace. We will fail others and ourselves. We will not always come to work with the best motives and intentions.

And, as a loving Father who delights in us, our Father God will faithfully deal with us in those moments. He will show us ways we have not trusted him. We might even have to take the consequences of our actions for a while as part of his discipline. But the discipline can lead to healing. As Hebrews continued to say:

> *"For the moment all discipline seems painful rather than pleasant, but later it yields the peaceful fruit of righteousness to those who have been trained by it."* (Hebrews 12:11)

We must be a people who trust him even when disciplined in and by our work because God is doing a beautiful work of training in our lives through it.

The Obedient Son

This entire Proverbs 3:1-12 passage encourages us—generally—to place our trust in God, and this trust in God should follow us into our workplaces. But then it also shows us specific areas we ought to trust him—with our character, with our abilities, with our finances, and even when God disciplines us. I pray we would increasingly trust God with and in our work because our work matters. I hope this short book has helped shape your framework for how to see your work.

And if we are honest, we often struggle to trust God with our work. Sometimes we let our Christian character or convictions slip because we cannot believe they could be effective in our workplace. Sometimes we are filled with pride and begin thinking the wisdom, knowledge, or talents we apply at work come from within us rather than from God. Sometimes we fail to honor God with our finances because we get such strong feelings of security and importance from it. Sometimes we despise God's disciplinary training, especially the ways he challenges us in our work, and wish he would leave us alone. And sometimes, we flat out do not trust him with our work, so we take matter into our own hands and act out purely on our own understanding.

Because we know these things about ourselves, we rejoice in Jesus. It is not too hard to see him here in this passage. The Proverbs are (mostly) written by a father to his son. The father is a king, and the son a future king. The wisdom of the Proverbs is the pleading of a good Israelite king to Israel's future king—*Here is wisdom! Heed it!* Through the cross, Jesus became the King of Kings and Lord of Lords. On his way there, he became the Son who trusted his Father. He kept every word of his Father's will. He always did that which pleased the Father (John 8:29).

And Jesus did everything this passage demands. He trusted his Father by remembering his teaching and commandments (1). He trusted his Father by allowing steadfast love and faithfulness to guide him (3). He trusted his Father by leaning on God for his energy and strength to accomplish his work (7). He even trusted his Father with his finances, and certainly with the first of billions of disciples (9). And he trusted the Father enough not to despise the Lord's discipline and reproof when it rained down upon him on the cross, taking our judgment into his body.

All this is encouraging to us because Jesus also gained all the rewards the son in Proverbs 3:1-12 was promised. He acquired length of days, years of life, and peace (2). He found favor and good success forever before both God and man, especially since one day every knee will bow before him (4). He got healing in his flesh and refreshment in his bones when he rose from the dead and ascended to God (8). He entered back into glory, a place of plenty, bursting with wine (10). And when we trust him, we acquire his inheritance and position. We get what he got.

So no matter the quality of our work, we humbly recognize our work could never save us and that only through Christ's work can we be delivered. Because of his work, believers enter into the greatest unearned blessings of all time. Unearned by us, that is, but earned by the perfect Son who trusted his Father to the final degree of the cross. Amen!

Bonus Chapter: Work Hard When Hard

The sluggard does not plow in the autumn; he will seek at harvest and have nothing. (Proverbs 20:4, ESV)

The Good Life

Nearly everyone has a vision of the good life. We can all easily project out to our latter years. We all have an idea of the ideal future. It will look different for each one of us. I have different dreams and aspirations than you do, but there will be some common themes.

For instance, we would all likely like to have strong, vibrant, and healthy relationships with the people we love. For my part, I want to be surrounded by my wife, my children, my grandchildren, and even great-grandchildren when I go home to God. Or we might all wish for financial health. I do not mean wealth—we do not all have a vision of that—but responsible stewardship of our finances. Or we might want physical health. We are realistic about this desire. We know age and death get us all in the end. And we know some sicknesses are not preventable. But—especially in the ways we can control—we might crave good health. On and on the list could go. But we all have a vision of that good life. As we walk with God, that vision is adjusted.

For some of us, the vision has to be adjusted "downward." What I mean is that many of us have visions of power and prosperity and fame that have nothing to do with Christ and his kingdom. So God must steadily adjust our vision until it becomes what he hopes for our lives.

But for some of us, our vision must be adjusted "upward." What I mean is that Christ must help us develop a better and more hopeful vision. Many human beings have been so discouraged by their past and conditioned by their environment that they fail to think any good could come of their lives. So Jesus might help this person dream of a life they never thought imaginable.

The Old Testament, Agrarian Perspective

The original audience of the Proverbs were the ancient Israelites, and they had a definite vision of the good life. There are many words that could describe their vision, but if you had to pick one word from our passage in this chapter, it might be the word "harvest."

Remember, their society lived off the land. Agriculture and livestock were in their blood, and God had brought them to a land flowing with milk and honey. Milk, because many cattle and goats and other livestock would thrive there. Honey, because bees would busily pollinate that which grew there.

For them, the vision of the good life was one of harvest. But our proverb paints an unfortunate picture: *"The sluggard does not plow in the autumn; he will seek at harvest and have nothing."*

It is a simple proverb to understand. Because the sluggard did not want to work during the autumn, he found no harvest in the spring. He would not plow and plant when the weather was bad, so he would not enjoy any fruit when the time came. He might have had a vision for the good life. He might have wanted a harvest. But he got none because he did not plow in the autumn.

Everyone Loves a Harvest

What No One Ever Says

In thinking about this verse, we must confess that everyone loves a good harvest. It is a rewarding experience to quietly and steadily work toward a goal and then experience the payoff. For Israel, it was a joy to eat and drink to the full because of a good harvest. Everyone loves it when life is good.

No one ever dreams of the non-harvest life. No one dreams of being an outcast by others. No one craves hostility in their closest relationships. No one wants financial ruin. No one longs for a fruitless ministry or life. No! Everyone loves a harvest.

A Life Plan

A few years ago, I tried something I hoped would help me develop a godly vision of what the harvest life would look like for Nate Holdridge. At the encouragement of Michael Hyatt's *Living Forward*, I created a document called a Life Plan.

The life plan exercise begins with writing your own eulogy. The idea is to write down what you hope they will say about you after you are gone. For instance, I had much in mine about my relationship with my wife and daughters. I also wrote a bit about my pastoral work—what I stood for, what I taught, and what I believed. And I had portions about my character because I want to live a godly life all the way through to the end of life.

After writing my eulogy, I then broke my life up into eight or nine categories—my spirit, my body, my marriage, my children, my key relationships, my work, and so on. Then I wrote under each heading what I envisioned for the future. It forced me to think through how each category is doing today and what I must do to improve them for tomorrow.

Accounts For Harvest

You might not spend much time and detail fleshing out your "harvest life," but it is healthy to allow the Spirit to craft a vision for where you are going. As you do, think of the different accounts or categories where you would like to see a harvest. Dream about your relationship with God, your relationships with others, your career goals, your friendships, and on and on. These are the areas you want to see harvests in. In each, you will want life and health. You will want a harvest. Everyone loves a harvest.

Not Everyone Loves Plowing in Autumn

The Hard Time

But not everyone loves plowing in the autumn. Let me show you what I mean. In Israel, "the autumn" was the time to plow and plant. Some translations say "the winter." The idea is that the farmer was bound to face some difficult weather. Conditions were not ideal. It would be hard to go out and plow the field during the autumn, but that was the time it needed to be done.

We likely already knew that hard work precedes a harvest. Someone has to till and plow and plant and water and weed and work to get a harvest.

WHOLE-HEARTED WORK

In a similar way, we know harvests in our life accounts are also preceded by preparatory work. Before a healthy savings account comes financial discipline. Before a good career comes an education. Before a loving family comes dedication, commitment, and care. Before a healthy marriage comes communication, faithfulness, and forgiveness. Before a fruitful ministry comes prayer and consecration.

Our Autumns

Here's the thing, it is all hard work. And sometimes, the conditions of life make it tempting to skip out on the painful work. It is easier to leave a marriage than fight for it. It is easier to drop out than struggle for your degree. It is easier to neglect your family than it is to learn how to love them. It is easier to quit the ministry than to war for God's people.

But when we are in the autumn, we must work. We must work hard when it is hard—and then the harvests of life will come.

This is one reason I believe physical exercise is an important practice for people in developed nations like ours. We can get by with a sedentary existence. But pushing yourself with exercise or physical training can help you learn how to work hard when it is hard.

I am on to different physical and athletic pursuits nowadays, but I spent my thirties involved in the sport of trail running. I was never fast. I was never a top runner. Do not get the wrong idea. It was just amateurish fun. But I got myself to the point I was able to complete a handful of marathons and ultra-marathons in a reasonable time.

And one thing I learned through the training runs and race days was that you have to run when it is hard to do so. I could not skip out when it rained, when it was cold, when it was dark, or when I did not feel like doing it. If I did, there was no way I could finish on race day. To get the harvest of finishing a race, I had to grind through the hard days of training.

This lesson has carried over to everyday life. I have learned to have hard conversations with my wife, even when I do not feel like it. I have learned to engage with my daughters even when it does not come naturally to me. I have learned to study and read, even when other things vie for my attention. I have learned—and am still learning—how to push through the desire to quit.

I am learning how to plow in the autumn.

So everyone loves harvest, though not everyone loves plowing in the autumn. But we must plow if we expect to live a harvest life.

Jesus Plowed in Autumn

At this point, it did not take a Christian pastor to write this chapter. God has written the law of the universe in such a way that anyone could observe that you gotta work to get a harvest.

Everyone knows this to one degree or another. We might be tempted by diet pills that offer us the figure we want without any work, but in the back of our minds, we know it is too good to be true. We know the $75 an hour job working from home ads are a scam. We know.

So even nonbelievers say things like, "no pain, no gain." "Just do it," says Nike, knowing the reward comes after the hard work. We know we must work hard when hard to get harvests in life. It does not take Jesus or the gospel or the Bible to know that.

How Jesus Helps Us Work Hard

What I have discovered is that I become capable of plowing in the autumn—I become able to work hard when it is hard—because of Jesus. He is the One who enables me to do the hard work when no one is watching. And he can enable you as well. Here's how:

First, Jesus himself plowed in autumn so that he could receive a harvest. What do I mean? Jesus was not a farmer, but he did reap a harvest of souls. In fact, the harvests of physical crops are likely meant to point us to the true harvest of souls at the end of the age. As Hebrews says, Jesus did everything he did to bring "many to glory" (Hebrews 2:10).

But for Jesus to save your soul or my soul, he had to work hard when it was hard. He had to become one of us, divesting himself of the privileges of his deity. He had to incarnate and live as a man. And then he had to suffer the agony of the cross. He had to die in our place so he could wash away our sins by his blood. And Jesus' cross was the hardest work anyone has ever done or will do. That was his autumn, and he worked during that hard time. And thank God that he did because it led to the great harvest. Now, through the gospel, people can be rejoined with God. People can be saved.

But Jesus is more than our example of hard work when hard. He also comes to live inside his people by his Spirit. The Spirit of Christ within us can strengthen us to work hard like Jesus, even when it is costly or painful to do so.

Some people are driven by nature. I am not. But when Christ came into my life and charged me up by his Spirit, something changed. As I have spent time with him, as I have worshipped him daily, he has transformed me to become more like himself. I still battle the temptation towards laziness, but he has deposited his work ethic into my soul. He has helped me work hard when hard by the power of his Spirit within me.

Brothers and sisters, the sluggard still looks for harvests where they never plowed, but we must plow. The world is filled with people who want great lives without any work involved. But there is no easy money. Instead, the Christian wants to be Christlike and work hard even when it is hard.

Harvests Beget Harvests

Allow me to end this chapter and book in two ways. First, let me encourage you. Second, let me tell you a secret.

Let me encourage you to work hard when it is hard. I know life is rough. There are pains involved. And there are circumstances way outside of your control. But, by the power of Christ, you can work hard when life is hard. And this will lead to a harvest in your life.

When I was a teenager, I had acne. Like many other pubescent boys, I did not like it. But I remember my mother told me to wash my face, apply anti-acne soap, and wait. As I grew, she assured me, it would all clear up. And she was right. As time passed, as my body developed, and as God made me a baritone, the acne cleared up.

This is like what you watch happen when you work hard when hard. Slowly, almost imperceptibly, you will discover life clearing up. Over time, the bills will not be so hard to pay. The relationships will not be so volatile. The kids will not be so disobedient. The work will not feel so overwhelming. Slowly, you will have grown, and you will enjoy the fruit of walking with God.

Now for the secret: harvests beget more harvests. Just as ancient farmers got seeds for their next crops from the previous harvests, so will your little victories and harvests turn into more.

Let me give you an example. One sentence from my eulogy I referred to earlier says, *"Thousands of younger men have believed God for their lives as a result of Nate's example and instruction."* I hope and pray this becomes the truth. I hope to die with many thousands of men celebrating that they were exposed to my life or teaching.

But, to get there, little harvests beget more harvests. For instance, one day, years ago, I decided to write a book for young men (*The No-Nonsense Biblical Man*). I did not think it would go far. I did not have big dreams for it, but I wanted to write down what I thought a godly man looked like so that others could follow. And that little harvest—getting that book done and published—has led to many more harvests as I have gotten many chances to influence young men for Christ. It was one step of thousands, one mini-harvest, that has led to more harvests.

You see, it is not all about how life ends. I mean, it is good to have that harvest-life image in your mind. But that life is not all suffering and pain and autumn-plowing-hard-work. No, this life of working for a harvest is a joy because there are thousands of mini-harvests along the way. And those mini-harvests lead to more harvests, so work hard when life is hard, and watch God produce his great blessings in your life.

Select Bibliography And Recommended Reading

Every Good Endeavor: Connecting Your Work to God's Work by Tim Keller

The Gospel & Work by Russell Moore

Work: A Kingdom Perspective by Ben Witherington

Business For The Glory Of God by Wayne Grudem

A Christian Perspective On Work And The Economy by Greg Forster

Margin by Richard A. Swenson

EntreLeadership by Dave Ramsey

Deep Work by Cal Newport

Other Nate Holdridge Resources

Books

The No-Nonsense Biblical Man

Dear New Dad

Let Us Hear: Studies on the Seven Letters of Revelation 2-3

Christ Unites: How Jesus Connects His People To His Purpose—a study of Ephesians

nateholdridge.com/books

Podcasts

Jesus Famous Podcast

Through The Bible Series Podcasts

Dear New Dad Podcast

Calvary Monterey Podcast

nateholdridge.com/podcasts

Blog

nateholdridge.com/blog

nateholdridge.com/subscribe